50 Japanese Soup Recipes for Home

By: Kelly Johnson

Table of Contents

- Miso Soup
- Tonjiru (Pork Soup)
- Kenchin-jiru (Vegetable Soup)
- Ozoni (New Year Mochi Soup)
- Ramen Soup
- Shoyu Ramen
- Tonkotsu Ramen
- Miso Ramen
- Shio Ramen
- Udon Noodle Soup
- Kitsune Udon
- Tempura Udon
- Nabeyaki Udon
- Soba Noodle Soup
- Kake Soba
- Tempura Soba
- Tanuki Soba
- Chawanmushi (Savory Egg Custard)
- Zosui (Rice Soup)
- Chazuke (Tea Rice Soup)
- Kabocha (Pumpkin) Soup
- Tofu and Wakame Soup
- Nikujaga (Meat and Potato Soup)
- Clear Clam Soup
- Clear Mushroom Soup
- Salmon Head Soup
- Crab Soup
- Fish Head Soup
- Shrimp Soup
- Tori Zosui (Chicken Rice Soup)
- Tamago Soup (Egg Drop Soup)
- Ankake Soup
- Sukiyaki Soup
- Niku Jaga Soup
- Daikon Soup

- Mochi Soup
- Tsukimi Udon
- Hoto Noodles Soup
- Shabu Shabu Soup
- Sumo Stew (Chanko Nabe)
- Oden
- Yudofu (Hot Tofu Soup)
- Yosenabe (Mixed Hot Pot)
- Kiritanpo Nabe
- Kimchi Nabe
- Tofu Miso Soup
- Gyoza Soup
- Age-dashi Tofu Soup
- Satsuma-jiru (Satsuma Soup)
- Hamaguri Ushio-jiru (Clam Soup)

Miso Soup

Ingredients:

- 4 cups dashi (Japanese soup stock)
- 3-4 tablespoons miso paste (white or red)
- 1/2 cup tofu, cut into small cubes
- 1/4 cup sliced green onions
- 1/4 cup wakame (dried seaweed), rehydrated
- Optional: mushrooms, spinach, or other vegetables

Instructions:

1. **Prepare the Dashi:**
    - In a pot, bring 4 cups of dashi to a gentle simmer over medium heat.
2. **Add Tofu and Wakame:**
    - Add the cubed tofu and rehydrated wakame to the pot. Simmer for about 2-3 minutes until the tofu is heated through.
3. **Mix Miso Paste:**
    - In a small bowl, take a ladleful of the hot dashi and mix it with the miso paste until it dissolves. This helps to prevent clumping.
4. **Combine Miso and Dashi:**
    - Slowly add the miso mixture back into the pot with the dashi and tofu. Stir gently to combine. Be careful not to let the soup boil once the miso is added, as boiling can cause the miso to lose its flavor and beneficial properties.
5. **Add Green Onions:**
    - Add the sliced green onions to the soup. Simmer for another minute.
6. **Serve:**
    - Ladle the soup into bowls and serve hot. Enjoy your traditional Japanese Miso Soup!

This basic recipe can be customized by adding ingredients like mushrooms, spinach, or other vegetables to suit your taste.

Tonjiru (Pork Soup)

Ingredients:

- 4 cups dashi (Japanese soup stock)
- 200g pork belly, thinly sliced
- 1 carrot, sliced into thin rounds
- 1 daikon radish, peeled and sliced into thin rounds
- 1 potato, peeled and cut into bite-sized pieces
- 1 onion, sliced
- 1/2 block of tofu, cut into cubes
- 1/4 cup miso paste
- 2 tablespoons soy sauce
- 1 tablespoon sake
- 1 tablespoon mirin
- 1 tablespoon sesame oil
- 2 green onions, sliced
- 1 teaspoon grated ginger

Instructions:

1. **Prepare the Ingredients:**
    - Slice the pork belly thinly.
    - Slice the carrot and daikon radish into thin rounds.
    - Peel and cut the potato into bite-sized pieces.
    - Slice the onion.
    - Cut the tofu into cubes.
2. **Sauté the Pork and Vegetables:**
    - In a large pot, heat the sesame oil over medium heat.
    - Add the sliced pork belly and grated ginger. Sauté until the pork is lightly browned.
    - Add the sliced onion, carrot, daikon radish, and potato. Sauté for a few minutes until the vegetables are slightly softened.
3. **Add Dashi:**
    - Pour in the dashi and bring the mixture to a simmer.
4. **Simmer the Soup:**
    - Add the tofu cubes to the pot.
    - Simmer for about 15-20 minutes, until the vegetables are tender and the flavors are well combined.
5. **Mix Miso Paste:**
    - In a small bowl, take a ladleful of the hot soup and mix it with the miso paste until it dissolves. This helps to prevent clumping.
6. **Combine Miso and Soup:**
    - Slowly add the miso mixture back into the pot. Stir gently to combine.
    - Add the soy sauce, sake, and mirin to the pot. Stir to combine.
7. **Add Green Onions:**
    - Add the sliced green onions to the soup. Simmer for another minute.
8. **Serve:**
    - Ladle the soup into bowls and serve hot. Enjoy your hearty and flavorful Tonjiru!

Kenchin-jiru (Vegetable Soup)

Ingredients:

- 4 cups dashi (Japanese soup stock)
- 1 block of tofu, cut into small cubes
- 1 carrot, sliced into thin rounds
- 1 daikon radish, peeled and sliced into thin rounds
- 1 potato, peeled and cut into bite-sized pieces
- 1 burdock root (gobo), thinly sliced
- 4 shiitake mushrooms, sliced
- 1/2 konnyaku (yam cake), sliced into thin pieces
- 2 tablespoons soy sauce
- 1 tablespoon miso paste
- 1 tablespoon sesame oil
- 2 green onions, sliced
- 1 teaspoon grated ginger
- Optional: spinach or other leafy greens

Instructions:

1. **Prepare the Ingredients:**
   - Cut the tofu into small cubes.
   - Slice the carrot and daikon radish into thin rounds.
   - Peel and cut the potato into bite-sized pieces.
   - Thinly slice the burdock root (gobo) after scrubbing it clean.
   - Slice the shiitake mushrooms.
   - Slice the konnyaku (yam cake) into thin pieces.
2. **Sauté the Vegetables:**
   - In a large pot, heat the sesame oil over medium heat.
   - Add the grated ginger and sauté briefly until fragrant.
   - Add the sliced burdock root, carrot, daikon radish, potato, shiitake mushrooms, and konnyaku. Sauté for a few minutes until the vegetables are slightly softened.
3. **Add Dashi:**
   - Pour in the dashi and bring the mixture to a simmer.
4. **Simmer the Soup:**
   - Add the tofu cubes to the pot.
   - Simmer for about 15-20 minutes, until the vegetables are tender and the flavors are well combined.
5. **Mix Miso Paste:**
   - In a small bowl, take a ladleful of the hot soup and mix it with the miso paste until it dissolves. This helps to prevent clumping.
6. **Combine Miso and Soup:**
   - Slowly add the miso mixture back into the pot. Stir gently to combine.
   - Add the soy sauce to the pot. Stir to combine.
7. **Add Green Onions:**
   - Add the sliced green onions to the soup. Simmer for another minute.
   - If using spinach or other leafy greens, add them at this stage and simmer until just wilted.
8. **Serve:**

- Ladle the soup into bowls and serve hot. Enjoy your nourishing and hearty Kenchin-jiru!

Ozoni (New Year Mochi Soup)

Ingredients:

- 4 cups dashi (Japanese soup stock)
- 4 pieces mochi (rice cakes)
- 1 chicken thigh, cut into bite-sized pieces
- 1 carrot, sliced into rounds
- 1 daikon radish, sliced into rounds
- 4 shiitake mushrooms, sliced
- 1/2 block of tofu, cut into cubes
- 1/2 bunch of spinach or mizuna, cut into bite-sized pieces
- 2 tablespoons soy sauce
- 1 tablespoon mirin
- 1 teaspoon salt
- 2 green onions, sliced
- Optional: yuzu peel or mitsuba (Japanese parsley) for garnish

Instructions:

1. **Prepare the Ingredients:**
    - Cut the chicken thigh into bite-sized pieces.
    - Slice the carrot and daikon radish into rounds.
    - Slice the shiitake mushrooms.
    - Cut the tofu into cubes.
    - Cut the spinach or mizuna into bite-sized pieces.
    - Slice the green onions.
2. **Toast the Mochi:**
    - Toast the mochi pieces under a broiler or in a toaster oven until they puff up and become slightly golden. Set aside.
3. **Cook the Chicken and Vegetables:**
    - In a large pot, bring the dashi to a simmer over medium heat.
    - Add the chicken pieces and simmer until they are cooked through, skimming off any foam that rises to the surface.
    - Add the sliced carrot, daikon radish, and shiitake mushrooms. Simmer for about 10 minutes until the vegetables are tender.
4. **Add Tofu and Seasonings:**
    - Add the tofu cubes to the pot.
    - Season the soup with soy sauce, mirin, and salt. Stir to combine and simmer for another 5 minutes.
5. **Add Greens and Mochi:**
    - Add the spinach or mizuna to the pot and simmer until just wilted.
    - Add the toasted mochi pieces to the pot and simmer for a minute or two until they soften.
6. **Serve:**
    - Ladle the soup into bowls, ensuring each serving has a piece of mochi, chicken, and vegetables.
    - Garnish with sliced green onions and, if desired, yuzu peel or mitsuba.
    - Serve hot and enjoy your traditional New Year Ozoni!

Ramen Soup

Ingredients:

- 4 cups chicken or pork broth
- 2-3 tablespoons soy sauce
- 1 tablespoon miso paste (optional)
- 1 tablespoon sake
- 1 tablespoon mirin
- 2 cloves garlic, minced
- 1-inch piece of ginger, minced
- 2 green onions, sliced (white and green parts separated)
- 2 eggs
- 200g fresh ramen noodles
- 100g sliced pork belly or chashu
- 1 cup bean sprouts
- 1 cup sliced mushrooms (shiitake or enoki)
- 1 sheet nori (seaweed), cut into strips
- 1/2 cup corn kernels
- 1 small bunch of spinach or bok choy
- Sesame oil for drizzling

Instructions:

1. **Prepare the Broth:**
   - In a large pot, combine the chicken or pork broth, soy sauce, miso paste (if using), sake, and mirin.
   - Add the minced garlic and ginger, and the white parts of the green onions.
   - Bring to a simmer over medium heat and let it cook gently for about 10-15 minutes to allow the flavors to meld.
2. **Cook the Eggs:**
   - Bring a small pot of water to a boil.
   - Carefully add the eggs and boil for 7 minutes for soft-boiled eggs.
   - Remove the eggs and place them in an ice bath to cool.
   - Once cool, peel the eggs and set them aside.
3. **Prepare the Noodles:**
   - Cook the ramen noodles according to the package instructions.
   - Drain and set aside.
4. **Prepare the Toppings:**
   - If using pork belly or chashu, heat a small amount of oil in a pan and sear the slices until they are lightly browned and heated through.
   - Blanch the spinach or bok choy in boiling water for 1-2 minutes until just tender. Drain and set aside.
5. **Assemble the Ramen Bowls:**
   - Divide the cooked ramen noodles among the serving bowls.
   - Pour the hot broth over the noodles.
   - Arrange the sliced pork belly or chashu, bean sprouts, mushrooms, corn, and blanched spinach or bok choy on top of the noodles.
   - Halve the soft-boiled eggs and place one half in each bowl.

- Garnish with the green parts of the green onions and nori strips.
- Drizzle a small amount of sesame oil over each bowl.
6. **Serve:**
   - Serve the ramen hot and enjoy your delicious homemade ramen soup!

Shoyu Ramen

Ingredients:

- 4 cups chicken or pork broth
- 1/4 cup soy sauce
- 1 tablespoon sake
- 1 tablespoon mirin
- 1 teaspoon sugar
- 2 cloves garlic, minced
- 1-inch piece of ginger, minced
- 2 green onions, sliced (white and green parts separated)
- 2 eggs
- 200g fresh ramen noodles
- 100g sliced pork belly or chashu
- 1 cup bean sprouts
- 1 cup sliced mushrooms (shiitake or enoki)
- 1 sheet nori (seaweed), cut into strips
- 1/2 cup corn kernels
- 1 small bunch of spinach or bok choy
- Sesame oil for drizzling

Instructions:

1. **Prepare the Broth:**
   - In a large pot, combine the chicken or pork broth, soy sauce, sake, mirin, and sugar.
   - Add the minced garlic, ginger, and the white parts of the green onions.
   - Bring to a simmer over medium heat and let it cook gently for about 10-15 minutes to allow the flavors to meld.
2. **Cook the Eggs:**
   - Bring a small pot of water to a boil.
   - Carefully add the eggs and boil for 7 minutes for soft-boiled eggs.
   - Remove the eggs and place them in an ice bath to cool.
   - Once cool, peel the eggs and set them aside.
3. **Prepare the Noodles:**
   - Cook the ramen noodles according to the package instructions.
   - Drain and set aside.
4. **Prepare the Toppings:**
   - If using pork belly or chashu, heat a small amount of oil in a pan and sear the slices until they are lightly browned and heated through.
   - Blanch the spinach or bok choy in boiling water for 1-2 minutes until just tender. Drain and set aside.
5. **Assemble the Ramen Bowls:**
   - Divide the cooked ramen noodles among the serving bowls.
   - Pour the hot broth over the noodles.
   - Arrange the sliced pork belly or chashu, bean sprouts, mushrooms, corn, and blanched spinach or bok choy on top of the noodles.
   - Halve the soft-boiled eggs and place one half in each bowl.
   - Garnish with the green parts of the green onions and nori strips.

- Drizzle a small amount of sesame oil over each bowl.
6. **Serve:**
    - Serve the ramen hot and enjoy your delicious homemade Shoyu Ramen!

Tonkotsu Ramen

Ingredients:

- 4 cups pork bone broth (homemade or store-bought)
- 1/4 cup soy sauce
- 2 tablespoons sake
- 1 tablespoon mirin
- 1 teaspoon sugar
- 2 cloves garlic, minced
- 1-inch piece of ginger, minced
- 2 green onions, sliced (white and green parts separated)
- 2 eggs
- 200g fresh ramen noodles
- 100g chashu pork (braised pork belly)
- 1 cup bean sprouts
- 1 cup sliced mushrooms (shiitake or enoki)
- 1 sheet nori (seaweed), cut into strips
- 1/2 cup corn kernels
- 1 small bunch of spinach or bok choy
- 1 tablespoon lard or pork fat (optional)
- Sesame oil for drizzling

Instructions:

1. **Prepare the Broth:**
   - In a large pot, combine the pork bone broth, soy sauce, sake, mirin, and sugar.
   - Add the minced garlic, ginger, and the white parts of the green onions.
   - Bring to a simmer over medium heat and let it cook gently for about 10-15 minutes to allow the flavors to meld.
   - If desired, add the lard or pork fat to enrich the broth.
2. **Cook the Eggs:**
   - Bring a small pot of water to a boil.
   - Carefully add the eggs and boil for 7 minutes for soft-boiled eggs.
   - Remove the eggs and place them in an ice bath to cool.
   - Once cool, peel the eggs and set them aside.
3. **Prepare the Noodles:**
   - Cook the ramen noodles according to the package instructions.
   - Drain and set aside.
4. **Prepare the Toppings:**
   - Heat a small amount of oil in a pan and sear the chashu pork slices until they are lightly browned and heated through.
   - Blanch the spinach or bok choy in boiling water for 1-2 minutes until just tender. Drain and set aside.
5. **Assemble the Ramen Bowls:**
   - Divide the cooked ramen noodles among the serving bowls.
   - Pour the hot broth over the noodles.
   - Arrange the chashu pork, bean sprouts, mushrooms, corn, and blanched spinach or bok choy on top of the noodles.

- Halve the soft-boiled eggs and place one half in each bowl.
- Garnish with the green parts of the green onions and nori strips.
- Drizzle a small amount of sesame oil over each bowl.

6. **Serve:**
    - Serve the ramen hot and enjoy your rich and flavorful Tonkotsu Ramen!

Miso Ramen

Ingredients:

- 4 cups chicken or pork broth
- 3 tablespoons miso paste (red or white)
- 1 tablespoon soy sauce
- 1 tablespoon sake
- 1 tablespoon mirin
- 2 cloves garlic, minced
- 1-inch piece of ginger, minced
- 2 green onions, sliced (white and green parts separated)
- 2 eggs
- 200g fresh ramen noodles
- 100g sliced pork belly or chashu
- 1 cup bean sprouts
- 1 cup sliced mushrooms (shiitake or enoki)
- 1 sheet nori (seaweed), cut into strips
- 1/2 cup corn kernels
- 1 small bunch of spinach or bok choy
- Sesame oil for drizzling
- 1 tablespoon butter (optional)

Instructions:

1. **Prepare the Broth:**
    - In a large pot, combine the chicken or pork broth, miso paste, soy sauce, sake, mirin, minced garlic, minced ginger, and the white parts of the green onions.
    - Bring to a simmer over medium heat and let it cook gently for about 10-15 minutes to allow the flavors to meld.
    - Add butter if desired for a richer flavor.
2. **Cook the Eggs:**
    - Bring a small pot of water to a boil.
    - Carefully add the eggs and boil for 7 minutes for soft-boiled eggs.
    - Remove the eggs and place them in an ice bath to cool.
    - Once cool, peel the eggs and set them aside.
3. **Prepare the Noodles:**
    - Cook the ramen noodles according to the package instructions.
    - Drain and set aside.
4. **Prepare the Toppings:**
    - If using pork belly or chashu, heat a small amount of oil in a pan and sear the slices until they are lightly browned and heated through.
    - Blanch the spinach or bok choy in boiling water for 1-2 minutes until just tender. Drain and set aside.
5. **Assemble the Ramen Bowls:**
    - Divide the cooked ramen noodles among the serving bowls.
    - Pour the hot broth over the noodles.
    - Arrange the sliced pork belly or chashu, bean sprouts, mushrooms, corn, and blanched spinach or bok choy on top of the noodles.

- Halve the soft-boiled eggs and place one half in each bowl.
 - Garnish with the green parts of the green onions and nori strips.
 - Drizzle a small amount of sesame oil over each bowl.
6. **Serve:**
 - Serve the ramen hot and enjoy your delicious homemade Miso Ramen!

Shio Ramen

Ingredients:

- 4 cups chicken or pork broth
- 2 tablespoons sea salt
- 1 tablespoon sake
- 1 tablespoon mirin
- 1 teaspoon sugar
- 2 cloves garlic, minced
- 1-inch piece of ginger, minced
- 2 green onions, sliced (white and green parts separated)
- 2 eggs
- 200g fresh ramen noodles
- 100g sliced pork belly or chashu
- 1 cup bean sprouts
- 1 cup sliced mushrooms (shiitake or enoki)
- 1 sheet nori (seaweed), cut into strips
- 1/2 cup corn kernels
- 1 small bunch of spinach or bok choy
- 1 teaspoon sesame oil
- Lemon wedges (optional)

Instructions:

1. **Prepare the Broth:**
   - In a large pot, combine the chicken or pork broth, sea salt, sake, mirin, sugar, minced garlic, minced ginger, and the white parts of the green onions.
   - Bring to a simmer over medium heat and let it cook gently for about 10-15 minutes to allow the flavors to meld.
2. **Cook the Eggs:**
   - Bring a small pot of water to a boil.
   - Carefully add the eggs and boil for 7 minutes for soft-boiled eggs.
   - Remove the eggs and place them in an ice bath to cool.
   - Once cool, peel the eggs and set them aside.
3. **Prepare the Noodles:**
   - Cook the ramen noodles according to the package instructions.
   - Drain and set aside.
4. **Prepare the Toppings:**
   - If using pork belly or chashu, heat a small amount of oil in a pan and sear the slices until they are lightly browned and heated through.
   - Blanch the spinach or bok choy in boiling water for 1-2 minutes until just tender. Drain and set aside.
5. **Assemble the Ramen Bowls:**
   - Divide the cooked ramen noodles among the serving bowls.
   - Pour the hot broth over the noodles.
   - Arrange the sliced pork belly or chashu, bean sprouts, mushrooms, corn, and blanched spinach or bok choy on top of the noodles.
   - Halve the soft-boiled eggs and place one half in each bowl.

- Garnish with the green parts of the green onions and nori strips.
- Drizzle a small amount of sesame oil over each bowl.
- If desired, serve with a lemon wedge for an extra burst of flavor.

6. **Serve:**
   - Serve the ramen hot and enjoy your delicate and savory Shio Ramen!

Udon Noodle Soup

Ingredients:

- 4 cups dashi (Japanese soup stock)
- 200g udon noodles (fresh or dried)
- 1 tablespoon soy sauce
- 1 tablespoon mirin
- 1 tablespoon sake
- 1 teaspoon sugar
- 1 small piece kombu (dried kelp)
- 1 cup sliced shiitake mushrooms
- 1/2 cup sliced bamboo shoots (menma)
- 1/2 cup sliced green onions
- 1/2 cup firm tofu, cubed
- 1 sheet nori (seaweed), cut into strips
- Optional: 2 eggs, soft-boiled and halved

Instructions:

1. **Prepare the Dashi:**
    - In a pot, combine the dashi stock and kombu. Bring to a simmer over medium heat and let it steep for about 5 minutes.
    - Remove the kombu from the pot.
2. **Cook the Udon Noodles:**
    - Cook the udon noodles according to the package instructions.
    - Drain and set aside.
3. **Prepare the Soup Base:**
    - To the dashi stock, add soy sauce, mirin, sake, and sugar. Stir to combine and bring back to a simmer.
4. **Add Mushrooms and Tofu:**
    - Add the sliced shiitake mushrooms and cubed tofu to the simmering broth.
    - Cook for about 2-3 minutes until the mushrooms are tender and the tofu is heated through.
5. **Add Bamboo Shoots and Green Onions:**
    - Add the sliced bamboo shoots (menma) and green onions to the soup. Cook for another minute.
6. **Serve:**
    - Divide the cooked udon noodles into serving bowls.
    - Ladle the hot soup over the noodles, ensuring each bowl gets an equal amount of mushrooms, tofu, and bamboo shoots.
    - Garnish with nori strips.
    - If using, add a soft-boiled egg half to each bowl.
7. **Optional Garnish:**
    - You can sprinkle some shichimi togarashi (Japanese seven-spice blend) or sesame seeds on top for added flavor and texture.
8. **Serve:**
    - Serve the udon noodle soup hot and enjoy its comforting and savory flavors!

Kitsune Udon

Ingredients:

- 4 cups dashi (Japanese soup stock)
- 200g udon noodles (fresh or dried)
- 2 tablespoons soy sauce
- 1 tablespoon mirin
- 1 tablespoon sake
- 1 teaspoon sugar
- 1 small piece kombu (dried kelp)
- 1/2 cup sliced aburaage (fried tofu pouches)
- 1 cup sliced shiitake mushrooms
- 1/2 cup sliced green onions
- Optional: 2 eggs, soft-boiled and halved

Instructions:

1. **Prepare the Dashi:**
    - In a pot, combine the dashi stock and kombu. Bring to a simmer over medium heat and let it steep for about 5 minutes.
    - Remove the kombu from the pot.
2. **Cook the Udon Noodles:**
    - Cook the udon noodles according to the package instructions.
    - Drain and set aside.
3. **Prepare the Soup Base:**
    - To the dashi stock, add soy sauce, mirin, sake, and sugar. Stir to combine and bring back to a simmer.
4. **Prepare Aburaage (Fried Tofu Pouches):**
    - Rinse the sliced aburaage under hot water to remove excess oil.
    - Add the aburaage slices to the simmering broth. Let them heat through for a minute.
5. **Add Shiitake Mushrooms and Green Onions:**
    - Add the sliced shiitake mushrooms and green onions to the soup. Cook for another minute until the mushrooms are tender.
6. **Serve:**
    - Divide the cooked udon noodles into serving bowls.
    - Ladle the hot soup over the noodles, ensuring each bowl gets an equal amount of aburaage, mushrooms, and green onions.
    - If using, add a soft-boiled egg half to each bowl.
7. **Optional Garnish:**
    - You can garnish Kitsune Udon with some shredded nori (seaweed) or sprinkle with shichimi togarashi (Japanese seven-spice blend) for added flavor and spice.
8. **Serve:**
    - Serve Kitsune Udon hot and enjoy the delicious combination of savory broth, chewy udon noodles, and flavorful toppings!

Tempura Udon

Ingredients:

- 4 cups dashi (Japanese soup stock)
- 200g udon noodles (fresh or dried)
- 2 tablespoons soy sauce
- 1 tablespoon mirin
- 1 tablespoon sake
- 1 teaspoon sugar
- 1 small piece kombu (dried kelp)
- Assorted tempura (shrimp, vegetables like sweet potato, pumpkin, and bell pepper)
- 1 cup sliced green onions
- Optional: 2 eggs, soft-boiled and halved

Instructions:

1. **Prepare the Dashi:**
    - In a pot, combine the dashi stock and kombu. Bring to a simmer over medium heat and let it steep for about 5 minutes.
    - Remove the kombu from the pot.
2. **Cook the Udon Noodles:**
    - Cook the udon noodles according to the package instructions.
    - Drain and set aside.
3. **Prepare the Soup Base:**
    - To the dashi stock, add soy sauce, mirin, sake, and sugar. Stir to combine and bring back to a simmer.
4. **Prepare Tempura:**
    - Heat oil in a deep frying pan or pot.
    - Dip the assorted tempura items (shrimp, sweet potato, pumpkin, bell pepper) into tempura batter and fry until golden and crispy. Drain on paper towels.
5. **Add Green Onions:**
    - Add sliced green onions to the simmering soup. Cook for a minute until they are tender.
6. **Serve:**
    - Divide the cooked udon noodles into serving bowls.
    - Ladle the hot soup over the noodles, ensuring each bowl gets an equal amount of green onions.
    - Arrange the assorted tempura on top of the udon noodles.
    - If using, add a soft-boiled egg half to each bowl.
7. **Optional Garnish:**
    - You can garnish Tempura Udon with some shredded nori (seaweed) or sprinkle with shichimi togarashi (Japanese seven-spice blend) for added flavor and spice.
8. **Serve:**
    - Serve Tempura Udon hot and enjoy the delicious combination of crispy tempura and savory udon noodles in flavorful broth!

Nabeyaki Udon

Ingredients:

- 4 cups dashi (Japanese soup stock)
- 200g udon noodles (fresh or dried)
- 2 tablespoons soy sauce
- 1 tablespoon mirin
- 1 tablespoon sake
- 1 teaspoon sugar
- 1 small piece kombu (dried kelp)
- 1 chicken thigh, sliced thinly
- 4-6 shrimp, peeled and deveined
- 1 cup sliced shiitake mushrooms
- 1 cup spinach leaves
- 1 small carrot, julienned
- 1/2 cup sliced bamboo shoots (menma)
- 1 sheet nori (seaweed), cut into strips
- 2 eggs
- 1 tablespoon vegetable oil
- Salt and pepper to taste

Instructions:

1. **Prepare the Dashi:**
   - In a pot, combine the dashi stock and kombu. Bring to a simmer over medium heat and let it steep for about 5 minutes.
   - Remove the kombu from the pot.
2. **Prepare the Udon Noodles:**
   - Cook the udon noodles according to the package instructions.
   - Drain and set aside.
3. **Prepare the Soup Base:**
   - To the dashi stock, add soy sauce, mirin, sake, and sugar. Stir to combine and bring back to a simmer.
4. **Cook the Chicken and Shrimp:**
   - Season the chicken slices and shrimp with salt and pepper.
   - In a separate pan, heat vegetable oil over medium heat.
   - Add the chicken slices and shrimp. Cook until the chicken is no longer pink and the shrimp turns pink and opaque. Remove from heat and set aside.
5. **Prepare Eggs:**
   - Bring a small pot of water to a boil.
   - Carefully add the eggs and boil for 7 minutes for soft-boiled eggs.
   - Remove the eggs and place them in an ice bath to cool.
   - Once cool, peel the eggs and set them aside.
6. **Assemble Nabeyaki Udon:**
   - In individual serving pots or bowls (nabe or donabe pots are traditional), divide the cooked udon noodles.
   - Arrange the cooked chicken, shrimp, sliced shiitake mushrooms, spinach leaves, julienned carrot, and bamboo shoots over the noodles.

7. **Add Soup Base:**
   - Pour the hot soup base over each serving, ensuring all ingredients are submerged.
8. **Add Eggs and Nori:**
   - Halve the soft-boiled eggs and place one half in each serving pot or bowl.
   - Garnish with nori strips on top.
9. **Serve:**
   - Serve Nabeyaki Udon hot, directly from the pot or bowl, and enjoy this hearty and flavorful Japanese noodle soup! Adjust seasoning with soy sauce or salt as desired.

Soba Noodle Soup

Ingredients:

- 4 cups dashi (Japanese soup stock)
- 200g soba noodles (buckwheat noodles)
- 2 tablespoons soy sauce
- 1 tablespoon mirin
- 1 tablespoon sake
- 1 teaspoon sugar
- 1 small piece kombu (dried kelp)
- 1 cup sliced shiitake mushrooms
- 1 cup spinach leaves
- 1/2 cup sliced green onions
- Optional: 2 eggs, soft-boiled and halved

Instructions:

1. **Prepare the Dashi:**
   - In a pot, combine the dashi stock and kombu. Bring to a simmer over medium heat and let it steep for about 5 minutes.
   - Remove the kombu from the pot.
2. **Cook the Soba Noodles:**
   - Cook the soba noodles according to the package instructions.
   - Drain and rinse well under cold water to remove excess starch. Set aside.
3. **Prepare the Soup Base:**
   - To the dashi stock, add soy sauce, mirin, sake, and sugar. Stir to combine and bring back to a simmer.
4. **Add Mushrooms and Spinach:**
   - Add the sliced shiitake mushrooms to the simmering soup. Cook for about 2-3 minutes until tender.
   - Add the spinach leaves and cook for another minute until wilted.
5. **Assemble Soba Noodle Soup:**
   - Divide the cooked soba noodles into serving bowls.
   - Ladle the hot soup over the noodles, ensuring each bowl gets an equal amount of mushrooms and spinach.
   - If using, add a soft-boiled egg half to each bowl.
6. **Garnish and Serve:**
   - Garnish with sliced green onions on top.
   - Serve Soba Noodle Soup hot and enjoy the comforting flavors of the broth and the nutty soba noodles!

This recipe is versatile, and you can adjust the toppings and seasonings to your taste preferences. Enjoy your homemade Soba Noodle Soup!

Kake Soba

Ingredients:

- 4 cups dashi (Japanese soup stock)
- 200g soba noodles (buckwheat noodles)
- 2 tablespoons soy sauce
- 1 tablespoon mirin
- 1 tablespoon sake
- 1 teaspoon sugar
- 1 small piece kombu (dried kelp)
- 1 cup sliced green onions (white and green parts separated)
- Optional: 2 eggs, soft-boiled and halved

Instructions:

1. **Prepare the Dashi:**
   - In a pot, combine the dashi stock and kombu. Bring to a simmer over medium heat and let it steep for about 5 minutes.
   - Remove the kombu from the pot.
2. **Cook the Soba Noodles:**
   - Cook the soba noodles according to the package instructions.
   - Drain and rinse well under cold water to remove excess starch. Set aside.
3. **Prepare the Soup Base:**
   - To the dashi stock, add soy sauce, mirin, sake, and sugar. Stir to combine and bring back to a simmer.
4. **Assemble Kake Soba:**
   - Divide the cooked soba noodles into serving bowls.
   - Ladle the hot soup over the noodles, ensuring each bowl gets an equal amount of broth.
   - If using, add a soft-boiled egg half to each bowl.
5. **Garnish and Serve:**
   - Garnish with sliced green onions (the green parts) on top.
   - Serve Kake Soba hot and enjoy the simple and flavorful Japanese noodle soup!

Kake Soba is known for its clean and light flavors, making it a comforting dish often enjoyed year-round in Japan. Adjust the seasonings according to your taste preferences and enjoy!

Tempura Soba

Ingredients:

- 4 cups dashi (Japanese soup stock)
- 200g soba noodles (buckwheat noodles)
- 2 tablespoons soy sauce
- 1 tablespoon mirin
- 1 tablespoon sake
- 1 teaspoon sugar
- 1 small piece kombu (dried kelp)
- Assorted tempura (shrimp, vegetables like sweet potato, pumpkin, and bell pepper)
- 1 cup sliced green onions (white and green parts separated)
- Optional: 2 eggs, soft-boiled and halved

Instructions:

1. **Prepare the Dashi:**
    - In a pot, combine the dashi stock and kombu. Bring to a simmer over medium heat and let it steep for about 5 minutes.
    - Remove the kombu from the pot.
2. **Cook the Soba Noodles:**
    - Cook the soba noodles according to the package instructions.
    - Drain and rinse well under cold water to remove excess starch. Set aside.
3. **Prepare the Soup Base:**
    - To the dashi stock, add soy sauce, mirin, sake, and sugar. Stir to combine and bring back to a simmer.
4. **Prepare Tempura:**
    - Heat oil in a deep frying pan or pot.
    - Dip the assorted tempura items (shrimp, sweet potato, pumpkin, bell pepper) into tempura batter and fry until golden and crispy. Drain on paper towels.
5. **Assemble Tempura Soba:**
    - Divide the cooked soba noodles into serving bowls.
    - Ladle the hot soup over the noodles, ensuring each bowl gets an equal amount of broth.
    - Arrange the assorted tempura on top of the soba noodles.
6. **Garnish and Serve:**
    - Garnish with sliced green onions (the green parts) on top.
    - If using, add a soft-boiled egg half to each bowl.
    - Serve Tempura Soba hot and enjoy the delightful combination of crispy tempura and savory soba noodles in flavorful broth!

This dish combines the heartiness of tempura with the lightness of soba noodles and dashi broth, making it a satisfying and delicious meal. Adjust the toppings and seasonings according to your taste preferences.

Tanuki Soba

Ingredients:

- 4 cups dashi (Japanese soup stock)
- 200g soba noodles (buckwheat noodles)
- 2 tablespoons soy sauce
- 1 tablespoon mirin
- 1 tablespoon sake
- 1 teaspoon sugar
- 1 small piece kombu (dried kelp)
- 1 cup sliced green onions (white and green parts separated)
- Tempura batter bits (crispy fried batter pieces)

Instructions:

1. **Prepare the Dashi:**
   - In a pot, combine the dashi stock and kombu. Bring to a simmer over medium heat and let it steep for about 5 minutes.
   - Remove the kombu from the pot.
2. **Cook the Soba Noodles:**
   - Cook the soba noodles according to the package instructions.
   - Drain and rinse well under cold water to remove excess starch. Set aside.
3. **Prepare the Soup Base:**
   - To the dashi stock, add soy sauce, mirin, sake, and sugar. Stir to combine and bring back to a simmer.
4. **Assemble Tanuki Soba:**
   - Divide the cooked soba noodles into serving bowls.
   - Ladle the hot soup over the noodles, ensuring each bowl gets an equal amount of broth.
5. **Add Tempura Batter Bits:**
   - Sprinkle crispy tempura batter bits generously over each bowl of soba noodles and broth.
6. **Garnish and Serve:**
   - Garnish with sliced green onions (the green parts) on top.
   - Serve Tanuki Soba hot and enjoy the delicious contrast of crispy tempura bits with the savory soba noodles and flavorful dashi broth!

Tanuki Soba is a popular dish in Japan known for its crunchy texture from the tempura bits and the comforting flavors of the soba noodles in the dashi broth. Adjust the seasonings and toppings to your liking and enjoy this simple yet satisfying meal!

Chawanmushi (Savory Egg Custard)

Ingredients:

- 2 cups dashi (Japanese soup stock)
- 3 large eggs
- 1 tablespoon soy sauce
- 1 tablespoon mirin
- 1/2 teaspoon salt
- 1/2 teaspoon sugar
- 4 medium shrimp, peeled and deveined
- 4 shiitake mushrooms, thinly sliced
- 4 slices kamaboko (Japanese fish cake)
- 2 tablespoons frozen green peas
- Optional: thinly sliced green onions or mitsuba (Japanese parsley) for garnish

Instructions:

1. **Prepare the Dashi:**
   - In a saucepan, heat the dashi over medium heat until warm. Remove from heat and let it cool slightly.
2. **Prepare the Custard Mixture:**
   - In a mixing bowl, beat the eggs gently without creating bubbles.
   - Gradually add warm dashi to the eggs, stirring constantly.
   - Add soy sauce, mirin, salt, and sugar. Mix well until everything is combined and the sugar and salt are dissolved.
3. **Prepare the Ingredients:**
   - Divide the shrimp, shiitake mushrooms, kamaboko slices, and green peas evenly among 4 small chawanmushi cups or heatproof bowls.
4. **Assemble and Steam:**
   - Pour the egg mixture through a fine-mesh sieve into each cup or bowl, covering the ingredients.
   - Cover each cup or bowl with aluminum foil or a lid.
5. **Steam the Chawanmushi:**
   - Prepare a steamer and bring water to a simmer.
   - Place the cups or bowls in the steamer and steam over medium-low heat for about 15-20 minutes, or until the custard is set but still slightly jiggly in the center.
6. **Serve:**
   - Carefully remove the chawanmushi from the steamer.
   - Garnish with thinly sliced green onions or mitsuba, if desired.
   - Serve Chawanmushi hot as an appetizer or side dish, and enjoy the delicate flavors and silky texture of this traditional Japanese savory egg custard!

Chawanmushi is a delicate dish that showcases the flavors of the ingredients within a silky smooth custard. Adjust the ingredients according to your preference and enjoy this classic Japanese dish at home!

Zosui (Rice Soup)

Ingredients:

- 4 cups dashi (Japanese soup stock)
- 2 cups cooked Japanese short-grain rice (preferably day-old)
- 2 eggs, beaten
- 1 tablespoon soy sauce
- 1 tablespoon mirin
- 1 tablespoon sake
- 1/2 teaspoon salt, or to taste
- 1 cup cooked chicken, shredded (or use leftover cooked meat such as beef or pork)
- 1 cup mixed vegetables (such as spinach, carrots, mushrooms, etc.)
- Optional: thinly sliced green onions for garnish

Instructions:

1. **Prepare the Dashi:**
    - In a pot, bring the dashi stock to a simmer over medium heat.
2. **Add Rice and Vegetables:**
    - Add the cooked rice to the simmering dashi. Stir gently to break up any clumps of rice.
    - Add the mixed vegetables and cooked chicken (or other meats). Cook until the vegetables are tender, about 5-7 minutes.
3. **Season the Soup:**
    - In a small bowl, mix together the beaten eggs, soy sauce, mirin, sake, and salt.
    - Slowly pour the egg mixture into the pot in a steady stream while gently stirring the soup with chopsticks or a spoon. This will create egg ribbons in the soup.
4. **Simmer:**
    - Continue to simmer the soup for another 2-3 minutes, stirring gently, until the eggs are fully cooked and the soup thickens slightly.
5. **Serve:**
    - Ladle the hot Zosui into serving bowls.
    - Garnish with thinly sliced green onions, if desired.
    - Serve Zosui hot as a comforting and nourishing dish, perfect for colder days or as a soothing meal after enjoying other Japanese dishes!

Zosui is versatile and can be adapted with various ingredients based on what you have on hand. Enjoy this hearty Japanese rice soup as a delicious way to use up leftover rice and create a satisfying meal.

Chazuke (Tea Rice Soup)

Ingredients:

- 2 cups cooked Japanese short-grain rice (preferably day-old)
- 2 cups hot green tea (sencha or genmaicha)
- 1 tablespoon soy sauce
- 1 tablespoon mirin
- 1 tablespoon sake
- 1 teaspoon grated ginger (optional)
- Nori (seaweed) strips, for garnish
- Optional toppings: pickled plum (umeboshi), toasted sesame seeds, thinly sliced green onions, grilled salmon or trout fillet, shredded nori

Instructions:

1. **Prepare the Tea:**
    - Brew 2 cups of hot green tea (sencha or genmaicha) in a teapot or using tea bags. Set aside.
2. **Prepare the Seasoning Sauce:**
    - In a small bowl, mix together soy sauce, mirin, sake, and grated ginger (if using). Set aside.
3. **Assemble Chazuke:**
    - Divide the cooked rice into serving bowls.
    - Pour hot green tea over the rice until it just covers the rice.
4. **Season the Soup:**
    - Drizzle the seasoning sauce over the rice and tea mixture.
5. **Add Toppings:**
    - Garnish with nori strips, pickled plum (umeboshi), toasted sesame seeds, thinly sliced green onions, and any other desired toppings.
6. **Serve:**
    - Serve Chazuke immediately while hot. Mix the rice and tea together as you eat, adjusting the seasoning and adding more tea or soy sauce mixture if desired.

Chazuke is a comforting and versatile dish that can be enjoyed as a light meal, a snack, or even a soothing remedy for an upset stomach. Experiment with different toppings and variations to suit your taste preferences!

Kabocha (Pumpkin) Soup

Ingredients:

- 1 small kabocha squash (about 2-3 pounds)
- 1 onion, chopped
- 2 cloves garlic, minced
- 4 cups vegetable or chicken broth
- 1 cup coconut milk
- 1 tablespoon olive oil
- 1 tablespoon curry powder
- 1/2 teaspoon ground cinnamon
- Salt and pepper, to taste
- Optional toppings: toasted pumpkin seeds, drizzle of coconut milk, chopped fresh cilantro

Instructions:

1. **Prepare the Kabocha Squash:**
    - Preheat the oven to 400°F (200°C).
    - Cut the kabocha squash in half and remove the seeds.
    - Place the squash halves cut-side down on a baking sheet lined with parchment paper.
    - Roast in the oven for 40-45 minutes, or until the squash is tender and easily pierced with a fork.
    - Remove from the oven and let it cool slightly. Scoop out the flesh and discard the skin. Set aside.
2. **Cook the Soup Base:**
    - In a large pot, heat olive oil over medium heat.
    - Add chopped onion and cook until translucent, about 5 minutes.
    - Add minced garlic, curry powder, and ground cinnamon. Cook for another 1-2 minutes until fragrant.
3. **Blend and Simmer:**
    - Add the roasted kabocha squash flesh to the pot.
    - Pour in vegetable or chicken broth and bring to a boil.
    - Reduce heat to low and simmer for 15-20 minutes to allow flavors to meld together.
4. **Blend the Soup:**
    - Use an immersion blender to blend the soup until smooth. Alternatively, carefully transfer the soup in batches to a blender and blend until smooth. Be cautious with hot liquids.
5. **Add Coconut Milk:**
    - Stir in coconut milk to the blended soup. Adjust the consistency with more broth or water if desired.
6. **Season and Serve:**
    - Season with salt and pepper to taste.
    - Ladle the soup into serving bowls.
    - Garnish with toasted pumpkin seeds, a drizzle of coconut milk, and chopped fresh cilantro if desired.
7. **Serve:**
    - Serve Kabocha Soup hot and enjoy the creamy, comforting flavors of this nutritious pumpkin soup!

Kabocha Soup is rich, creamy, and slightly sweet, making it a perfect warming dish for cooler weather. Adjust the seasonings and toppings according to your preference.

Tofu and Wakame Soup

Ingredients:

- 4 cups dashi (Japanese soup stock)
- 1 block (about 14 oz) firm tofu, cut into small cubes
- 1/4 cup dried wakame seaweed, rehydrated in water and drained
- 2 tablespoons soy sauce
- 1 tablespoon mirin
- 1 tablespoon sake
- 1 teaspoon grated ginger
- 2 green onions, thinly sliced
- Optional: 1 egg, beaten (for egg drop style)

Instructions:

1. **Prepare the Dashi:**
    - In a pot, bring the dashi stock to a simmer over medium heat.
2. **Add Tofu and Wakame:**
    - Carefully add the tofu cubes and rehydrated wakame seaweed to the simmering dashi.
3. **Season the Soup:**
    - Add soy sauce, mirin, sake, and grated ginger to the soup. Stir gently to combine.
4. **Simmer:**
    - Allow the soup to simmer for about 5-7 minutes, or until the tofu is heated through and the flavors have melded together.
5. **Optional Egg Drop:**
    - If using the egg, slowly pour it into the simmering soup in a steady stream while gently stirring the soup. This will create egg ribbons.
6. **Finish and Serve:**
    - Remove the soup from heat.
    - Stir in thinly sliced green onions.
    - Ladle the hot Tofu and Wakame Soup into serving bowls.
7. **Serve:**
    - Serve Tofu and Wakame Soup hot as a comforting and nutritious dish, perfect for a light meal or as part of a Japanese-style meal.

This soup is light yet flavorful, showcasing the delicate flavors of tofu and wakame seaweed in a savory dashi broth. Adjust the seasonings to your taste preference and enjoy this traditional Japanese soup!

Nikujaga (Meat and Potato Soup)

Ingredients:

- 1 lb thinly sliced beef (such as ribeye or sirloin)
- 4 medium potatoes, peeled and cut into chunks
- 2 carrots, peeled and sliced
- 1 onion, thinly sliced
- 2 cups dashi (Japanese soup stock)
- 1/4 cup soy sauce
- 2 tablespoons mirin
- 1 tablespoon sugar
- 1 tablespoon vegetable oil
- Optional: 1 block firm tofu, cut into cubes
- Optional garnish: thinly sliced green onions or parsley

Instructions:

1. **Prepare the Beef:**
   - Heat vegetable oil in a large pot over medium heat.
   - Add thinly sliced beef and cook until browned.
2. **Add Vegetables:**
   - Add sliced onion, potatoes, and carrots to the pot with the beef. Stir to combine.
3. **Prepare the Seasoning:**
   - In a bowl, mix together dashi, soy sauce, mirin, and sugar until well combined.
4. **Simmer:**
   - Pour the seasoning mixture over the beef and vegetables in the pot.
   - Bring to a boil, then reduce heat to low. Cover and simmer for about 20-25 minutes, or until the potatoes are tender and cooked through.
5. **Optional Tofu Addition:**
   - If using tofu, gently add cubed tofu to the pot during the last 5 minutes of cooking.
6. **Adjust Seasoning:**
   - Taste and adjust seasoning with more soy sauce or sugar if desired.
7. **Serve:**
   - Serve Nikujaga hot, garnished with thinly sliced green onions or parsley if desired.
   - Enjoy this hearty and comforting Japanese stew with steamed rice!

Nikujaga is a classic Japanese comfort food dish, featuring tender beef, potatoes, and vegetables simmered in a savory-sweet sauce. Adjust the ingredients and seasonings to your taste preferences and enjoy this flavorful stew!

Clear Clam Soup

Ingredients:

- 1 lb fresh clams (such as littleneck or Manila clams), cleaned and scrubbed
- 4 cups dashi (Japanese soup stock)
- 1 tablespoon soy sauce
- 1 tablespoon mirin
- 1 tablespoon sake
- 1 teaspoon salt, or to taste
- 2 green onions, thinly sliced (for garnish)
- Optional: thinly sliced fresh ginger

Instructions:

1. **Prepare the Clams:**
   - Clean the clams thoroughly under cold running water to remove any sand or debris.
   - If using larger clams, such as Manila clams, scrub the shells with a brush.
2. **Cook the Clams:**
   - In a large pot, bring 2 cups of water to a boil.
   - Add the cleaned clams to the boiling water and cover the pot.
   - Steam the clams for about 5-7 minutes, or until they open.
   - Discard any clams that do not open.
3. **Prepare the Dashi:**
   - In a separate pot, bring the dashi stock to a simmer over medium heat.
4. **Combine Ingredients:**
   - Once the clams are cooked and removed from their shells (reserve a few in shells for garnish if desired), add them to the simmering dashi stock.
   - Add soy sauce, mirin, sake, and salt to the pot. Stir gently to combine.
5. **Simmer:**
   - Allow the soup to simmer for another 5 minutes to let the flavors meld together.
6. **Serve:**
   - Ladle the hot Clear Clam Soup into serving bowls.
   - Garnish with thinly sliced green onions and optionally, a few reserved clams in shells.
   - Serve the soup hot as a light and flavorful appetizer or part of a Japanese meal.

Clear Clam Soup is delicate and brimming with the natural sweetness of clams, enhanced by the umami flavors of dashi and seasonings. Enjoy this simple yet elegant soup as part of your Japanese culinary experience!

Clear Mushroom Soup

Ingredients:

- 4 cups vegetable or chicken broth
- 1 cup assorted fresh mushrooms (shiitake, button mushrooms, oyster mushrooms), sliced
- 1 small onion, thinly sliced
- 2 cloves garlic, minced
- 1 tablespoon soy sauce
- 1 tablespoon mirin
- 1 tablespoon sake (optional)
- Salt and pepper, to taste
- 2 tablespoons vegetable oil
- 2 green onions, thinly sliced (for garnish)
- Optional: thinly sliced ginger or a few drops of sesame oil for extra flavor

Instructions:

1. **Prepare the Mushrooms:**
    - Heat vegetable oil in a pot over medium heat.
    - Add minced garlic and sliced onion. Sauté until the onion becomes translucent, about 3-4 minutes.
2. **Cook the Mushrooms:**
    - Add sliced mushrooms to the pot. Sauté for another 5-6 minutes, or until the mushrooms are tender and lightly browned.
3. **Add Broth and Seasonings:**
    - Pour vegetable or chicken broth into the pot with the mushrooms.
    - Add soy sauce, mirin, and sake (if using).
    - Season with salt and pepper to taste.
    - Optionally, add thinly sliced ginger or a few drops of sesame oil for additional flavor.
4. **Simmer:**
    - Bring the soup to a boil, then reduce heat to low. Let it simmer uncovered for about 10-15 minutes to allow the flavors to meld together.
5. **Adjust Seasoning:**
    - Taste the soup and adjust seasoning if needed, adding more soy sauce, mirin, or salt according to your preference.
6. **Serve:**
    - Ladle the hot Clear Mushroom Soup into serving bowls.
    - Garnish with thinly sliced green onions.
    - Serve the soup hot as a light and flavorful starter or as part of a Japanese-themed meal.

This Clear Mushroom Soup is delicate yet flavorful, highlighting the earthy richness of fresh mushrooms in a savory broth. Enjoy its simplicity and comforting qualities with each spoonful!

Salmon Head Soup

Ingredients:

- 1 salmon head, cleaned and chopped into smaller pieces
- 8 cups water or fish stock
- 1 onion, chopped
- 2 carrots, peeled and sliced
- 2 celery stalks, sliced
- 2 cloves garlic, minced
- 1 tablespoon vegetable oil
- 1 bay leaf
- 1 teaspoon dried thyme (or a few sprigs of fresh thyme)
- Salt and pepper, to taste
- Optional: 1 tablespoon soy sauce or fish sauce for added depth
- Fresh parsley or dill, chopped (for garnish)

Instructions:

1. **Prepare the Salmon Head:**
   - Rinse the salmon head under cold water to remove any residual blood or impurities.
   - Chop the salmon head into smaller pieces, including the cheeks and the collar, which are particularly flavorful.
2. **Sauté Aromatics:**
   - Heat vegetable oil in a large pot over medium heat.
   - Add chopped onion, carrots, celery, and garlic. Sauté for about 5 minutes, or until the vegetables start to soften and become fragrant.
3. **Simmer the Soup:**
   - Add the chopped salmon head pieces to the pot.
   - Pour in water or fish stock, ensuring the salmon head is fully submerged.
   - Add bay leaf and dried thyme (or fresh thyme sprigs).
   - Season with salt and pepper to taste.
   - Optionally, add soy sauce or fish sauce for added depth of flavor.
4. **Cook the Soup:**
   - Bring the soup to a boil, then reduce heat to low and let it simmer gently for about 30-40 minutes. Skim any foam or impurities that rise to the surface during cooking.
5. **Serve:**
   - Once the soup is ready and the flavors have melded together, remove the bay leaf and thyme sprigs if using.
   - Ladle the hot Salmon Head Soup into serving bowls.
   - Garnish with fresh chopped parsley or dill.
6. **Enjoy:**
   - Serve the Salmon Head Soup hot, accompanied by crusty bread or rice if desired.

This soup captures the rich umami flavors of salmon and provides a comforting and nourishing dish, perfect for colder days or as a main course in a seafood-themed meal. Adjust the seasonings and ingredients according to your taste preferences for a personalized touch.

Crab Soup

Ingredients:

- 2-3 whole crabs (Dungeness or blue crab), cleaned and cracked
- 8 cups water or seafood stock
- 1 onion, chopped
- 2 celery stalks, chopped
- 2 carrots, peeled and sliced
- 2 cloves garlic, minced
- 1 tablespoon vegetable oil
- 1 bay leaf
- 1 teaspoon dried thyme (or a few sprigs of fresh thyme)
- Salt and pepper, to taste
- 1 cup heavy cream or coconut milk (optional, for a creamy soup)
- Fresh parsley or chives, chopped (for garnish)

Instructions:

1. **Prepare the Crabs:**
   - Clean the crabs thoroughly, removing any gills and washing off any sediment or debris.
   - Crack the crab shells to help release more flavor during cooking.
2. **Sauté Aromatics:**
   - Heat vegetable oil in a large pot over medium heat.
   - Add chopped onion, celery, carrots, and garlic. Sauté for about 5 minutes, or until the vegetables start to soften and become fragrant.
3. **Cook the Crab:**
   - Add the cracked crabs to the pot with the sautéed vegetables.
   - Pour in water or seafood stock, ensuring the crabs are fully submerged.
4. **Season and Simmer:**
   - Add bay leaf and dried thyme (or fresh thyme sprigs).
   - Season with salt and pepper to taste.
   - Bring the soup to a boil, then reduce heat to low and let it simmer gently for about 30-40 minutes. This allows the flavors from the crab to infuse into the broth.
5. **Optional Creamy Version:**
   - If desired, stir in heavy cream or coconut milk to create a creamy texture. Simmer for an additional 5-10 minutes to combine flavors.
6. **Serve:**
   - Once the soup is ready and the flavors have melded together, remove the bay leaf and thyme sprigs if using.
   - Ladle the hot Crab Soup into serving bowls.
   - Garnish with chopped fresh parsley or chives.
7. **Enjoy:**
   - Serve the Crab Soup hot, accompanied by crusty bread or a side of rice for a satisfying meal.

This Crab Soup recipe highlights the natural sweetness of crab meat and creates a comforting and nourishing soup that's perfect for seafood lovers. Adjust the seasonings and ingredients according to your taste preferences for a personalized touch.

Fish Head Soup

Ingredients:

- 2-3 fish heads (such as snapper, cod, or any white fish), cleaned and rinsed
- 8 cups water or fish stock
- 1 onion, chopped
- 2 carrots, peeled and sliced
- 2 celery stalks, chopped
- 2 cloves garlic, minced
- 1 tablespoon vegetable oil
- 1 bay leaf
- 1 teaspoon dried thyme (or a few sprigs of fresh thyme)
- Salt and pepper, to taste
- Optional: 1 cup coconut milk or heavy cream for a creamy version
- Fresh parsley or dill, chopped (for garnish)

Instructions:

1. **Prepare the Fish Heads:**
   - Rinse the fish heads under cold water to remove any blood or impurities.
   - Cut the fish heads into smaller pieces, ensuring they fit comfortably in your cooking pot.
2. **Sauté Aromatics:**
   - Heat vegetable oil in a large pot over medium heat.
   - Add chopped onion, carrots, celery, and garlic. Sauté for about 5 minutes, or until the vegetables begin to soften and become fragrant.
3. **Cook the Fish Heads:**
   - Add the fish heads to the pot with the sautéed vegetables.
   - Pour in water or fish stock, ensuring the fish heads are fully submerged.
4. **Season and Simmer:**
   - Add bay leaf and dried thyme (or fresh thyme sprigs).
   - Season with salt and pepper to taste.
   - Bring the soup to a boil, then reduce heat to low and let it simmer gently for about 30-40 minutes. This allows the flavors from the fish heads to infuse into the broth.
5. **Optional Creamy Version:**
   - For a creamy soup, stir in coconut milk or heavy cream. Simmer for an additional 5-10 minutes to blend the flavors together.
6. **Serve:**
   - Once the soup is ready and the fish heads have imparted their flavors into the broth, remove the bay leaf and thyme sprigs if using.
   - Ladle the hot Fish Head Soup into serving bowls.
   - Garnish with chopped fresh parsley or dill.
7. **Enjoy:**
   - Serve the Fish Head Soup hot, accompanied by crusty bread or steamed rice for a satisfying meal.

This Fish Head Soup recipe captures the essence of the fish heads' natural richness and creates a comforting and nourishing soup that's perfect for seafood enthusiasts. Adjust the seasonings and ingredients according to your preferences for a personalized touch.

Shrimp Soup

Ingredients:

- 1 lb shrimp, peeled and deveined (shells reserved for making broth, if desired)
- 8 cups water or seafood stock
- 1 onion, chopped
- 2 carrots, peeled and sliced
- 2 celery stalks, chopped
- 2 cloves garlic, minced
- 1 tablespoon vegetable oil
- 1 bay leaf
- 1 teaspoon dried thyme (or a few sprigs of fresh thyme)
- Salt and pepper, to taste
- Optional: 1 cup coconut milk or heavy cream for a creamy version
- Fresh parsley or cilantro, chopped (for garnish)
- Lime wedges (for serving)

Instructions:

1. **Prepare the Shrimp Broth (Optional):**
   - If using shrimp shells to make broth, heat vegetable oil in a large pot over medium heat.
   - Add shrimp shells and sauté until pink and fragrant, about 5-7 minutes.
   - Add water or seafood stock to the pot, bring to a boil, then reduce heat and simmer for 20-30 minutes. Strain and set aside.
2. **Sauté Aromatics:**
   - Heat vegetable oil in a large pot over medium heat.
   - Add chopped onion, carrots, celery, and garlic. Sauté for about 5 minutes, or until vegetables start to soften and become fragrant.
3. **Cook the Shrimp:**
   - Add peeled and deveined shrimp to the pot with sautéed vegetables.
   - Pour in water or seafood stock (or shrimp broth if using).
   - Add bay leaf and dried thyme (or fresh thyme sprigs).
   - Season with salt and pepper to taste.
4. **Simmer:**
   - Bring the soup to a boil, then reduce heat to low and let it simmer gently for about 5-7 minutes, or until shrimp are pink and cooked through.
5. **Optional Creamy Version:**
   - If desired, stir in coconut milk or heavy cream to create a creamy texture. Simmer for an additional 2-3 minutes to blend flavors.
6. **Serve:**
   - Once the soup is ready and flavors have melded together, remove the bay leaf and thyme sprigs if using.
   - Ladle the hot Shrimp Soup into serving bowls.
   - Garnish with chopped fresh parsley or cilantro.
   - Serve with lime wedges on the side for squeezing over the soup.
7. **Enjoy:**
   - Serve the Shrimp Soup hot, accompanied by crusty bread or steamed rice for a satisfying meal.

This Shrimp Soup recipe captures the natural sweetness of shrimp and creates a comforting and flavorful dish that's perfect for seafood lovers. Adjust the seasonings and ingredients according to your preferences for a personalized touch.

Tori Zosui (Chicken Rice Soup)

Ingredients:

- 2 boneless, skinless chicken breasts, thinly sliced
- 4 cups chicken broth
- 2 cups water
- 1 cup cooked rice (preferably short-grain rice)
- 1 carrot, thinly sliced
- 1/2 cup bamboo shoots, sliced (optional)
- 2 green onions, thinly sliced
- 1 tablespoon soy sauce
- 1 tablespoon mirin (Japanese sweet rice wine)
- 1 teaspoon sesame oil
- Salt and pepper, to taste
- 1 egg, beaten
- Fresh parsley or cilantro, chopped (for garnish)

Instructions:

1. **Prepare the Chicken and Vegetables:**
   - In a large pot, bring chicken broth and water to a simmer over medium heat.
   - Add thinly sliced chicken breasts, carrot slices, and bamboo shoots (if using). Cook for about 5-7 minutes, or until chicken is cooked through and vegetables are tender.
2. **Add Rice and Flavorings:**
   - Stir in cooked rice, green onions, soy sauce, mirin, and sesame oil. Mix well to combine.
   - Season with salt and pepper to taste. Adjust seasoning as needed.
3. **Simmer:**
   - Allow the soup to simmer gently for another 5-7 minutes to let the flavors meld together.
4. **Add Beaten Egg:**
   - Slowly pour the beaten egg into the simmering soup in a steady stream while gently stirring the soup. This will create egg ribbons throughout the soup.
5. **Finish and Serve:**
   - Once the egg is cooked and soup is heated through, remove from heat.
   - Ladle the hot Tori Zosui into serving bowls.
   - Garnish with chopped fresh parsley or cilantro.
6. **Enjoy:**
   - Serve Tori Zosui hot as a comforting and satisfying meal, perfect for chilly days or as a light dinner option.

Tori Zosui is a traditional Japanese rice soup that combines tender chicken, vegetables, and rice in a flavorful broth. Adjust the ingredients and seasonings according to your taste preferences for a personalized touch.

Tamago Soup (Egg Drop Soup)

Ingredients:

- 4 cups chicken broth or vegetable broth
- 3 eggs
- 2 tablespoons soy sauce
- 1 tablespoon mirin (Japanese sweet rice wine)
- 1 teaspoon grated ginger (optional)
- 2 green onions, thinly sliced
- Salt and white pepper, to taste
- 1 teaspoon sesame oil (optional)
- Fresh cilantro or parsley, chopped (for garnish)

Instructions:

1. **Prepare the Broth:**
   - In a medium pot, bring chicken broth or vegetable broth to a gentle simmer over medium heat.
2. **Season the Broth:**
   - Stir in soy sauce, mirin, and grated ginger (if using). Adjust seasoning with salt and white pepper to taste.
3. **Prepare the Eggs:**
   - In a small bowl, beat the eggs until well combined.
4. **Add Eggs to Broth:**
   - Slowly pour the beaten eggs into the simmering broth in a steady stream while stirring the soup gently with a fork or chopsticks. This will create egg ribbons throughout the soup.
5. **Finish and Serve:**
   - Once the eggs are cooked and soup is heated through (about 1-2 minutes), remove from heat.
   - Stir in sesame oil (if using) for added flavor.
6. **Garnish and Serve:**
   - Ladle the hot Tamago Soup into serving bowls.
   - Garnish with thinly sliced green onions and chopped cilantro or parsley.
7. **Enjoy:**
   - Serve Tamago Soup hot as a light and comforting appetizer or as part of a larger meal.

Tamago Soup is a quick and easy dish that's perfect for warming up on chilly days or as a soothing starter before a main course. Adjust the ingredients and seasonings according to your taste preferences for a personalized touch.

Ankake Soup

Ingredients:

- 4 cups chicken or vegetable broth
- 1 tablespoon soy sauce
- 1 tablespoon mirin (Japanese sweet rice wine)
- 1 teaspoon grated ginger
- 1 tablespoon cornstarch dissolved in 2 tablespoons water
- 1 cup mixed vegetables (such as carrots, mushrooms, bamboo shoots, and spinach), thinly sliced or chopped
- 1 cup cooked chicken, shrimp, or tofu, diced (optional)
- 2 green onions, thinly sliced (for garnish)
- Salt and pepper, to taste
- 1 tablespoon vegetable oil

Instructions:

1. **Prepare the Broth:**
    - In a medium pot, bring chicken or vegetable broth to a simmer over medium heat.
2. **Season the Broth:**
    - Stir in soy sauce, mirin, and grated ginger. Adjust seasoning with salt and pepper to taste.
3. **Add Vegetables and Protein (if using):**
    - Heat vegetable oil in a separate pan over medium heat.
    - Sauté mixed vegetables until slightly tender, about 3-4 minutes.
    - Add cooked chicken, shrimp, or tofu (if using) to the vegetables and cook until heated through.
4. **Thicken the Soup:**
    - Stir the cornstarch mixture to recombine, then gradually pour it into the simmering broth while stirring continuously.
    - Continue to simmer for 1-2 minutes, or until the soup thickens slightly.
5. **Finish and Serve:**
    - Divide the cooked vegetables and protein evenly among serving bowls.
    - Ladle the hot Ankake Soup over the vegetables and protein.
6. **Garnish and Serve:**
    - Garnish with thinly sliced green onions.
7. **Enjoy:**
    - Serve Ankake Soup hot as a flavorful and satisfying dish, perfect for a light lunch or dinner.

Ankake Soup offers a balance of savory flavors with a hint of sweetness from mirin, complemented by the umami-rich soy sauce and the freshness of grated ginger. Adjust the ingredients and protein choices according to your preferences for a personalized Ankake Soup experience.

Sukiyaki Soup

Ingredients:

- 4 cups dashi broth (Japanese fish and seaweed stock) or beef broth
- 1/3 cup soy sauce
- 1/3 cup mirin (Japanese sweet rice wine)
- 2 tablespoons sugar
- 1 tablespoon vegetable oil
- 1 onion, thinly sliced
- 1/2 lb thinly sliced beef (such as ribeye or sirloin)
- 1/2 lb firm tofu, cut into cubes
- 1/2 lb shiitake mushrooms, sliced
- 1 bunch spinach, washed and trimmed
- 4-5 green onions, cut into 2-inch lengths
- 1 package of shirataki noodles, rinsed and drained (optional)
- 2-3 eggs, beaten (for dipping)

Instructions:

1. **Prepare the Broth:**
    - In a large pot, combine dashi broth (or beef broth), soy sauce, mirin, and sugar. Bring to a simmer over medium heat.
2. **Sauté the Ingredients:**
    - Heat vegetable oil in a separate pan over medium-high heat.
    - Add thinly sliced onion and sauté until translucent, about 2-3 minutes.
    - Add thinly sliced beef to the pan and cook until browned, about 1-2 minutes.
3. **Combine Ingredients:**
    - Add the sautéed onion and beef to the simmering broth in the pot.
    - Add tofu cubes, sliced shiitake mushrooms, spinach, green onions, and shirataki noodles (if using). Simmer for about 5-7 minutes, or until vegetables are tender and flavors meld together.
4. **Serve:**
    - Ladle the hot Sukiyaki Soup into individual serving bowls.
    - Serve with beaten eggs in a separate bowl for dipping.
5. **Enjoy:**
    - To eat, dip cooked ingredients into the beaten eggs before enjoying. The eggs should be lightly cooked from the hot broth, adding a creamy texture to each bite.

Sukiyaki Soup is traditionally enjoyed as a communal dish where everyone dips the cooked ingredients into the beaten eggs before eating. Adjust the ingredients and seasonings according to your taste preferences for a personalized Sukiyaki Soup experience.

Niku Jaga Soup

Ingredients:

- 1 lb thinly sliced beef (such as ribeye or sirloin)
- 4 potatoes, peeled and cut into bite-sized pieces
- 1 onion, thinly sliced
- 2 carrots, peeled and sliced
- 4 cups dashi broth (Japanese fish and seaweed stock) or beef broth
- 1/3 cup soy sauce
- 1/3 cup mirin (Japanese sweet rice wine)
- 2 tablespoons sugar
- 1 tablespoon vegetable oil
- Salt and pepper, to taste
- 2-3 green onions, thinly sliced (for garnish)
- Steamed rice (for serving)

Instructions:

1. **Prepare the Ingredients:**
   - In a large pot, heat vegetable oil over medium-high heat.
   - Add thinly sliced beef and cook until browned, about 2-3 minutes.
2. **Add Vegetables:**
   - Add sliced onion and carrots to the pot with the beef. Sauté for another 2-3 minutes, until vegetables are slightly softened.
3. **Simmer with Broth:**
   - Pour dashi broth (or beef broth) into the pot with the beef and vegetables.
   - Stir in soy sauce, mirin, and sugar. Mix well to combine.
   - Add potato pieces to the pot. Bring the mixture to a boil, then reduce heat to low.
4. **Cook Until Tender:**
   - Simmer Niku Jaga Soup uncovered for about 20-25 minutes, or until potatoes are tender and flavors have melded together.
   - Season with salt and pepper to taste.
5. **Serve:**
   - Ladle the hot Niku Jaga Soup into serving bowls.
   - Garnish with thinly sliced green onions.
6. **Enjoy:**
   - Serve Niku Jaga Soup hot alongside steamed rice for a comforting and satisfying meal.

Niku Jaga Soup is perfect for colder days and offers a balance of sweet and savory flavors from the soy sauce, mirin, and sugar. Adjust the ingredients and seasonings according to your taste preferences for a personalized Niku Jaga Soup experience.

Daikon Soup

Ingredients:

- 1 medium daikon radish, peeled and thinly sliced
- 4 cups chicken or vegetable broth
- 1 tablespoon soy sauce
- 1 tablespoon mirin (Japanese sweet rice wine)
- 1 teaspoon grated ginger
- Salt and pepper, to taste
- 2 green onions, thinly sliced (for garnish)
- Optional: 1 teaspoon sesame oil

Instructions:

1. **Prepare the Daikon:**
   - Peel the daikon radish and slice it thinly. You can cut it into rounds or half-moons, depending on your preference.
2. **Simmer the Daikon:**
   - In a medium pot, bring chicken or vegetable broth to a simmer over medium heat.
   - Add the thinly sliced daikon radish to the pot.
3. **Season the Soup:**
   - Stir in soy sauce, mirin, and grated ginger.
   - Season with salt and pepper to taste.
   - Optionally, add sesame oil for additional flavor.
4. **Simmer Until Tender:**
   - Let the Daikon Soup simmer gently for about 15-20 minutes, or until the daikon radish slices are tender and cooked through.
5. **Serve:**
   - Ladle the hot Daikon Soup into serving bowls.
   - Garnish with thinly sliced green onions.
6. **Enjoy:**
   - Serve Daikon Soup hot as a comforting and nourishing dish, perfect for a light lunch or as a starter to a larger meal.

Daikon Soup highlights the mild, slightly sweet flavor of daikon radish, enhanced by the savory broth and aromatics like ginger and green onions. Adjust the seasonings and ingredients according to your taste preferences for a personalized Daikon Soup experience.

Mochi Soup

Ingredients:

- 4 cups dashi broth (Japanese fish and seaweed stock) or chicken broth
- 1/4 cup soy sauce
- 1 tablespoon mirin (Japanese sweet rice wine)
- 1 tablespoon sake (Japanese rice wine)
- 1 teaspoon sugar
- 4 pieces mochi (rice cakes)
- 1/2 lb chicken breast or thigh, thinly sliced (optional)
- 1 carrot, thinly sliced
- 1/2 cup shiitake mushrooms, sliced
- 2-3 green onions, thinly sliced (for garnish)
- Optional: 1 sheet nori (seaweed), cut into small pieces

Instructions:

1. **Prepare the Broth:**
   - In a large pot, combine dashi broth (or chicken broth), soy sauce, mirin, sake, and sugar. Bring to a simmer over medium heat.
2. **Add Ingredients:**
   - If using chicken, add thinly sliced chicken to the simmering broth and cook until chicken is cooked through.
   - Add carrot slices and shiitake mushrooms to the pot. Simmer for about 5 minutes, or until vegetables are tender.
3. **Prepare Mochi (Rice Cakes):**
   - Toast mochi over an open flame, grill, or in a toaster oven until they puff up and become slightly crispy on the outside. Alternatively, you can briefly microwave them until softened.
4. **Serve:**
   - Divide mochi among serving bowls.
   - Ladle the hot Mochi Soup (Ozoni) over the mochi and vegetables.
5. **Garnish and Serve:**
   - Garnish with thinly sliced green onions and nori pieces (if using).
6. **Enjoy:**
   - Serve Mochi Soup (Ozoni) hot as a traditional Japanese New Year's dish or as a comforting soup throughout the year.

Mochi Soup (Ozoni) is a flavorful and comforting dish that brings together the richness of mochi with the umami flavors of dashi broth and traditional Japanese seasonings. Adjust the ingredients and seasonings according to your taste preferences for a personalized Mochi Soup experience.

Tsukimi Udon

Ingredients:

- 4 cups dashi broth (Japanese fish and seaweed stock) or vegetable broth
- 2 tablespoons soy sauce
- 1 tablespoon mirin (Japanese sweet rice wine)
- 1 tablespoon sake (Japanese rice wine)
- 1 tablespoon sugar
- 2 packs (about 14 oz) udon noodles
- 4 eggs
- 2 green onions, thinly sliced (for garnish)
- Optional: Nori (seaweed) strips, for garnish

Instructions:

1. **Prepare the Broth:**
    - In a large pot, combine dashi broth (or vegetable broth), soy sauce, mirin, sake, and sugar. Bring to a simmer over medium heat.
2. **Cook Udon Noodles:**
    - Cook udon noodles according to package instructions. Drain and set aside.
3. **Poach the Eggs:**
    - Crack each egg into a small bowl or cup.
    - Bring a separate pot of water to a gentle simmer.
    - Carefully slide each egg into the simmering water and poach for about 3-4 minutes, until the whites are set but the yolks are still runny.
4. **Assemble the Tsukimi Udon:**
    - Divide cooked udon noodles among serving bowls.
    - Ladle the hot broth over the noodles, ensuring each bowl gets plenty of flavor.
5. **Add Poached Eggs:**
    - Carefully place one poached egg on top of each bowl of udon noodles and broth.
6. **Garnish and Serve:**
    - Garnish Tsukimi Udon with thinly sliced green onions and nori strips (if using).
7. **Enjoy:**
    - Serve Tsukimi Udon hot as a comforting and hearty noodle soup, with the poached egg representing the moon floating in the broth.

Tsukimi Udon is a delightful dish that combines the simplicity of udon noodles with the richness of a savory broth and the creamy texture of a poached egg. Adjust the seasonings and garnishes according to your taste preferences for a personalized Tsukimi Udon experience.

Hoto Noodles Soup

Ingredients:

- 8 cups water
- 4 cups dashi broth (Japanese fish and seaweed stock)
- 1 tablespoon soy sauce
- 1 tablespoon miso paste
- 1 tablespoon sake (Japanese rice wine)
- 1 tablespoon mirin (Japanese sweet rice wine)
- 1 tablespoon vegetable oil
- 1 onion, thinly sliced
- 2 carrots, peeled and sliced
- 1/2 medium daikon radish, peeled and sliced
- 2 potatoes, peeled and cut into bite-sized pieces
- 1/2 kabocha squash, peeled, seeds removed, and cut into bite-sized pieces (optional)
- 1 pack (about 14 oz) thick udon noodles
- Salt and pepper, to taste
- Green onions, thinly sliced (for garnish)
- Toasted sesame seeds (for garnish)

Instructions:

1. **Prepare the Broth:**
   - In a large pot, combine water and dashi broth. Bring to a boil over medium-high heat.
2. **Season the Broth:**
   - Reduce heat to medium-low. Stir in soy sauce, miso paste, sake, and mirin until miso paste is dissolved and ingredients are well combined.
3. **Add Vegetables:**
   - Heat vegetable oil in a separate pan over medium heat.
   - Add thinly sliced onion and sauté until translucent, about 2-3 minutes.
   - Add carrots, daikon radish, potatoes, and kabocha squash (if using) to the pan. Sauté for another 5 minutes, stirring occasionally.
4. **Cook the Noodles:**
   - Add udon noodles to the pot of boiling broth. Cook according to package instructions, typically 8-10 minutes, until noodles are tender but still chewy.
5. **Combine and Simmer:**
   - Add sautéed vegetables to the pot of broth and noodles. Stir gently to combine.
   - Simmer Hoto Noodles Soup for another 5-7 minutes, allowing flavors to meld together and vegetables to become tender.
6. **Adjust Seasoning:**
   - Season Hoto Noodles Soup with salt and pepper to taste.
7. **Serve:**
   - Ladle the hot Hoto Noodles Soup into serving bowls.
   - Garnish with thinly sliced green onions and toasted sesame seeds.
8. **Enjoy:**
   - Serve Hoto Noodles Soup hot as a comforting and nourishing meal, perfect for chilly days or when you crave a hearty noodle soup.

Hoto Noodles Soup is known for its robust flavors and variety of vegetables, making it a satisfying dish on its own. Adjust the ingredients and seasonings according to your taste preferences for a personalized Hoto Noodles Soup experience.

Shabu Shabu Soup

Ingredients:

- 6 cups dashi broth (Japanese fish and seaweed stock) or beef broth
- 1/4 cup soy sauce
- 1/4 cup mirin (Japanese sweet rice wine)
- 1 tablespoon sake (Japanese rice wine)
- 1 tablespoon sugar
- 1/2 lb thinly sliced beef (such as ribeye or sirloin)
- Assorted vegetables (such as napa cabbage, spinach, carrots, mushrooms, and green onions), thinly sliced or cut into bite-sized pieces
- 1 block tofu, cut into cubes
- 1 package shirataki noodles, rinsed and drained
- Cooked udon or soba noodles (optional)
- Dipping sauces (such as ponzu sauce, sesame sauce, or goma dare)
- Cooked rice (for serving)

Instructions:

1. **Prepare the Broth:**
    - In a large pot, combine dashi broth (or beef broth), soy sauce, mirin, sake, and sugar. Bring to a simmer over medium heat.
2. **Prepare Ingredients:**
    - Arrange thinly sliced beef, assorted vegetables, tofu cubes, and shirataki noodles on separate plates or bowls for easy access.
3. **Cooking Process:**
    - Each diner uses chopsticks to swish a piece of thinly sliced beef in the hot broth ("shabu shabu" motion), cooking it briefly until just done. Remove cooked beef and dip in preferred dipping sauce before eating.
    - Repeat with assorted vegetables, tofu, and shirataki noodles, cooking each in the broth until tender.
4. **Serve:**
    - Serve Shabu Shabu Soup with cooked rice on the side.
    - Enjoy with dipping sauces and additional garnishes like green onions or grated daikon radish.
5. **Enjoy:**
    - Shabu Shabu Soup is enjoyed as a communal meal where each diner cooks their ingredients at the table, creating a personalized and interactive dining experience.

Shabu Shabu Soup is a delightful dish that highlights the freshness of ingredients and the richness of the broth. Adjust the ingredients and dipping sauces according to your taste preferences for a personalized Shabu Shabu Soup experience.

Sumo Stew (Chanko Nabe)

Ingredients:

- 8 cups dashi broth (Japanese fish and seaweed stock) or chicken broth
- 1/2 cup soy sauce
- 1/2 cup mirin (Japanese sweet rice wine)
- 1/4 cup sake (Japanese rice wine)
- 2 tablespoons sugar
- 1 lb chicken thighs, thinly sliced
- 1 lb firm tofu, cut into cubes
- 1 lb napa cabbage, cut into bite-sized pieces
- 1 bunch spinach, washed and trimmed
- 1 daikon radish, peeled and thinly sliced
- 4-6 shiitake mushrooms, sliced
- 1 block konnyaku (yam cake), sliced into thin rounds
- 1 bunch enoki mushrooms, roots trimmed
- 4 green onions, thinly sliced (for garnish)
- Cooked udon noodles or rice (optional, for serving)

Instructions:

1. **Prepare the Broth:**
   - In a large pot, combine dashi broth (or chicken broth), soy sauce, mirin, sake, and sugar. Bring to a simmer over medium heat.
2. **Add Protein and Vegetables:**
   - Add thinly sliced chicken thighs to the simmering broth and cook until chicken is cooked through, about 5-7 minutes.
   - Add tofu cubes, napa cabbage, spinach, daikon radish, shiitake mushrooms, konnyaku, and enoki mushrooms to the pot. Simmer for another 10-15 minutes, or until vegetables are tender.
3. **Serve:**
   - Ladle the hot Sumo Stew (Chanko Nabe) into individual serving bowls.
   - Garnish with thinly sliced green onions.
4. **Optional Serving:**
   - Serve Sumo Stew (Chanko Nabe) with cooked udon noodles or rice on the side, if desired.
5. **Enjoy:**
   - Sumo Stew (Chanko Nabe) is meant to be shared and enjoyed with others, providing a hearty and satisfying meal packed with nutritious ingredients.

Chanko Nabe is versatile, allowing you to adjust the ingredients and seasonings according to your taste preferences. It's a perfect dish for gatherings or when you crave a warming and nutritious hot pot experience.

Oden

Ingredients:

- 6 cups dashi broth (Japanese fish and seaweed stock)
- 1/2 cup soy sauce
- 1/4 cup mirin (Japanese sweet rice wine)
- 1 tablespoon sugar
- Assorted Oden ingredients (choose from the following):
    - Daikon radish, peeled and cut into thick rounds
    - Konnyaku (yam cake), sliced into rounds or triangles
    - Hard-boiled eggs, peeled
    - Atsuage (fried tofu), cut into thick slices
    - Hanpen (fish cake), cut into pieces
    - Chikuwa (fish cake tubes), cut into pieces
    - Gobo (burdock root), peeled and cut into pieces
    - Kabocha squash, peeled and cut into chunks
    - Boiled potatoes, peeled and cut into chunks
    - Slices of beef tendon (optional, for richer flavor)

Instructions:

1. **Prepare the Broth:**
    - In a large pot, combine dashi broth, soy sauce, mirin, and sugar. Bring to a simmer over medium heat.
2. **Add Oden Ingredients:**
    - Add daikon radish, konnyaku, eggs, atsuage, hanpen, chikuwa, gobo, kabocha squash, potatoes, and beef tendon (if using) to the pot.
3. **Simmer:**
    - Simmer Oden ingredients in the broth for about 30-40 minutes, or until vegetables are tender and flavors have melded together.
4. **Serve:**
    - Ladle the hot Oden and its broth into individual bowls or a large serving dish.
    - Optionally, serve with hot mustard or grated daikon radish as a condiment.
5. **Enjoy:**
    - Oden is traditionally enjoyed hot as a main dish or as a comforting winter meal. It's often served with a bowl of steamed rice or as part of a larger Japanese meal.

Oden is versatile, allowing you to customize the ingredients based on your preferences and what's available. The key is to simmer the ingredients gently in the flavorful broth until they absorb the savory flavors of the dashi and soy sauce. Adjust the seasonings and ingredients to create your own delicious Oden experience at home.

Yudofu (Hot Tofu Soup)

Ingredients:

- 1 block (about 14 oz) firm tofu, drained and cut into cubes
- 4 cups dashi broth (Japanese fish and seaweed stock) or vegetable broth
- 1/4 cup soy sauce
- 2 tablespoons mirin (Japanese sweet rice wine)
- 2 green onions, thinly sliced (for garnish)
- Optional: Shredded nori (seaweed) or grated ginger, for garnish

Instructions:

1. **Prepare the Broth:**
    - In a medium pot, combine dashi broth (or vegetable broth), soy sauce, and mirin. Bring to a gentle simmer over medium heat.
2. **Add Tofu:**
    - Carefully add tofu cubes to the simmering broth. Be gentle to avoid breaking the tofu cubes.
3. **Simmer:**
    - Let the Yudofu simmer gently for about 5-7 minutes, allowing the tofu to absorb the flavors of the broth.
4. **Serve:**
    - Ladle the hot Yudofu into individual serving bowls.
    - Garnish with thinly sliced green onions and shredded nori or grated ginger (if using).
5. **Enjoy:**
    - Serve Yudofu hot as a light and comforting soup, perfect for a chilly day or as a starter to a Japanese meal.

Yudofu emphasizes the clean and delicate flavor of tofu, complemented by the umami-rich dashi broth and the subtle sweetness of mirin. Adjust the seasonings according to your taste preferences, and feel free to add additional garnishes or ingredients like mushrooms or spinach for variation.

Yosenabe (Mixed Hot Pot)

Ingredients:

- 8 cups dashi broth (Japanese fish and seaweed stock) or chicken broth
- 1/4 cup soy sauce
- 1/4 cup mirin (Japanese sweet rice wine)
- 2 tablespoons sake (Japanese rice wine)
- 1 tablespoon sugar
- 1 lb thinly sliced chicken, beef, or pork (or a combination)
- 1/2 lb firm tofu, cut into cubes
- 1 napa cabbage, sliced into bite-sized pieces
- 1 bunch spinach, washed and trimmed
- 1 carrot, peeled and thinly sliced
- 1 daikon radish, peeled and thinly sliced
- 4-6 shiitake mushrooms, sliced
- 1 block konnyaku (yam cake), sliced into rounds
- 1 bunch enoki mushrooms, roots trimmed
- 1/2 package shirataki noodles, rinsed and drained
- 4 green onions, thinly sliced (for garnish)
- Cooked udon or soba noodles (optional, for serving)
- Dipping sauces (such as ponzu sauce or sesame sauce)

Instructions:

1. **Prepare the Broth:**
   - In a large pot, combine dashi broth (or chicken broth), soy sauce, mirin, sake, and sugar. Bring to a simmer over medium heat.
2. **Add Meat and Tofu:**
   - Add thinly sliced chicken, beef, or pork to the simmering broth. Cook until meat is cooked through, about 5-7 minutes.
   - Add tofu cubes to the pot and simmer for another 2-3 minutes.
3. **Add Vegetables and Mushrooms:**
   - Add napa cabbage, spinach, carrot, daikon radish, shiitake mushrooms, konnyaku, enoki mushrooms, and shirataki noodles to the pot.
   - Simmer Yosenabe for about 10-15 minutes, or until vegetables are tender and flavors have melded together.
4. **Serve:**
   - Ladle the hot Yosenabe and its broth into individual serving bowls or a large serving dish.
   - Garnish with thinly sliced green onions.
5. **Optional Serving:**
   - Serve Yosenabe with cooked udon or soba noodles on the side, if desired.
   - Provide dipping sauces like ponzu sauce or sesame sauce for extra flavor.
6. **Enjoy:**
   - Yosenabe is meant to be enjoyed hot as a communal meal, where diners cook their ingredients in the flavorful broth at the table. It's a comforting and nutritious dish perfect for gatherings or chilly evenings.

Yosenabe allows for flexibility in ingredients, so feel free to customize with your favorite meats, vegetables, and mushrooms. Adjust the seasonings and dipping sauces according to your taste preferences for a personalized Yosenabe experience at home.

Kiritanpo Nabe

Ingredients:

- 6 cups dashi broth (Japanese fish and seaweed stock)
- 1/4 cup soy sauce
- 1/4 cup mirin (Japanese sweet rice wine)
- 2 tablespoons sake (Japanese rice wine)
- 1 tablespoon sugar
- 1 lb chicken thighs, thinly sliced
- 4 kiritanpo sticks (store-bought or homemade, see below)
- 1 napa cabbage, sliced into bite-sized pieces
- 1 leek, sliced diagonally
- 4 shiitake mushrooms, sliced
- 1 carrot, peeled and sliced
- 1/2 block firm tofu, cut into cubes
- 1 bunch enoki mushrooms, roots trimmed
- 4 green onions, thinly sliced (for garnish)

For Kiritanpo Sticks (if making from scratch):

- 2 cups sushi rice
- Water
- Salt

Instructions:

1. **Prepare Kiritanpo Sticks (if making from scratch):**
    - Rinse sushi rice under cold water until the water runs clear. Drain well.
    - In a rice cooker or pot, cook the rice with slightly less water than usual to make it firm.
    - Once the rice is cooked, let it cool slightly. Wet your hands with water and sprinkle with salt. Shape the rice into cylindrical sticks around skewers or chopsticks.
    - Grill the sticks over an open flame or in a broiler until golden brown and crispy on the outside. Set aside.
2. **Prepare the Broth:**
    - In a large pot, combine dashi broth, soy sauce, mirin, sake, and sugar. Bring to a simmer over medium heat.
3. **Add Chicken and Vegetables:**
    - Add thinly sliced chicken thighs to the simmering broth. Cook until chicken is no longer pink, about 5-7 minutes.
    - Add napa cabbage, leek, shiitake mushrooms, carrot, tofu cubes, and enoki mushrooms to the pot. Simmer for another 10 minutes, or until vegetables are tender.
4. **Add Kiritanpo Sticks:**
    - Gently add grilled kiritanpo sticks to the pot. Let them simmer in the broth for about 5 minutes to absorb flavors.
5. **Serve:**
    - Ladle the hot Kiritanpo Nabe and its broth into individual serving bowls or a large serving dish.
    - Garnish with thinly sliced green onions.

6. **Enjoy:**
    - Kiritanpo Nabe is traditionally enjoyed hot as a main dish, perfect for colder months. Serve with rice or enjoy as is, savoring the flavors of the savory broth and grilled rice sticks.

Kiritanpo Nabe offers a comforting and rustic dining experience, showcasing the regional flavors of Akita Prefecture in Japan. Adjust the ingredients and seasonings according to your taste preferences for a personalized Kiritanpo Nabe at home.

Kimchi Nabe

Ingredients:

- 6 cups dashi broth (Japanese fish and seaweed stock) or chicken broth
- 1/2 cup kimchi, chopped
- 1/4 cup kimchi juice (from the jar of kimchi)
- 1/4 cup soy sauce
- 2 tablespoons sake (Japanese rice wine)
- 1 tablespoon sesame oil
- 1 tablespoon sugar
- 1 lb thinly sliced pork belly or pork shoulder
- 1 block tofu, cut into cubes
- 1 napa cabbage, sliced into bite-sized pieces
- 1 leek, sliced diagonally
- 4 shiitake mushrooms, sliced
- 1 carrot, peeled and sliced
- 1/2 package shirataki noodles, rinsed and drained
- 4 green onions, thinly sliced (for garnish)
- Cooked rice or udon noodles (optional, for serving)

Instructions:

1. **Prepare the Broth:**
    - In a large pot, combine dashi broth (or chicken broth), kimchi, kimchi juice, soy sauce, sake, sesame oil, and sugar. Bring to a simmer over medium heat.
2. **Add Pork and Tofu:**
    - Add thinly sliced pork belly or pork shoulder to the simmering broth. Cook until pork is no longer pink, about 5-7 minutes.
    - Add tofu cubes to the pot. Simmer for another 2-3 minutes.
3. **Add Vegetables and Noodles:**
    - Add napa cabbage, leek, shiitake mushrooms, carrot, and shirataki noodles to the pot.
    - Simmer Kimchi Nabe for about 10-15 minutes, or until vegetables are tender and flavors have melded together.
4. **Serve:**
    - Ladle the hot Kimchi Nabe and its broth into individual serving bowls or a large serving dish.
    - Garnish with thinly sliced green onions.
5. **Optional Serving:**
    - Serve Kimchi Nabe with cooked rice or udon noodles on the side, if desired.
6. **Enjoy:**
    - Kimchi Nabe is meant to be enjoyed hot as a communal meal. The spicy and tangy flavors of kimchi complement the savory broth and tender pork, creating a comforting and satisfying dish perfect for gatherings or cold evenings.

Kimchi Nabe allows for flexibility in ingredients and spice levels, so adjust the amount of kimchi and kimchi juice according to your preference for spiciness. Serve with additional kimchi on the side for those who enjoy extra heat.

Tofu Miso Soup

Ingredients:

- 4 cups dashi broth (Japanese fish and seaweed stock) or vegetable broth
- 1/4 cup miso paste (white or red, according to preference)
- 1 block (about 14 oz) firm tofu, cut into small cubes
- 2 green onions, thinly sliced
- Optional: Wakame seaweed, soaked in water and drained (about 1/4 cup)

Instructions:

1. **Prepare the Broth:**
   - In a medium pot, bring dashi broth (or vegetable broth) to a gentle simmer over medium heat.
2. **Dissolve Miso Paste:**
   - In a small bowl, add miso paste. Ladle a small amount of hot broth into the bowl with miso paste and whisk until miso paste is completely dissolved and smooth.
3. **Add Tofu and Wakame:**
   - Add tofu cubes and optional soaked wakame seaweed to the simmering broth. Cook for about 2-3 minutes, or until tofu is heated through and seaweed is tender.
4. **Flavor Adjustment:**
   - Reduce heat to low. Add dissolved miso paste to the pot, stirring gently to combine. Avoid boiling the soup once miso paste has been added, as it can affect the flavor.
5. **Serve:**
   - Ladle the hot Tofu Miso Soup into individual serving bowls.
   - Garnish with thinly sliced green onions.
6. **Enjoy:**
   - Tofu Miso Soup is traditionally enjoyed hot as a starter to a Japanese meal or as a comforting dish on its own. It's nutritious, flavorful, and versatile, allowing for customization with additional ingredients like mushrooms or spinach.

This recipe is simple yet flavorful, highlighting the clean taste of tofu combined with the savory richness of miso. Adjust the amount of miso paste according to your taste preferences for a milder or stronger miso flavor.

Gyoza Soup

Ingredients:

- 4 cups dashi broth (Japanese fish and seaweed stock) or vegetable broth
- 1/4 cup miso paste (white or red, according to preference)
- 1 block (about 14 oz) firm tofu, cut into small cubes
- 2 green onions, thinly sliced
- Optional: Wakame seaweed, soaked in water and drained (about 1/4 cup)

Instructions:

1. **Prepare the Broth:**
   - In a medium pot, bring dashi broth (or vegetable broth) to a gentle simmer over medium heat.
2. **Dissolve Miso Paste:**
   - In a small bowl, add miso paste. Ladle a small amount of hot broth into the bowl with miso paste and whisk until miso paste is completely dissolved and smooth.
3. **Add Tofu and Wakame:**
   - Add tofu cubes and optional soaked wakame seaweed to the simmering broth. Cook for about 2-3 minutes, or until tofu is heated through and seaweed is tender.
4. **Flavor Adjustment:**
   - Reduce heat to low. Add dissolved miso paste to the pot, stirring gently to combine. Avoid boiling the soup once miso paste has been added, as it can affect the flavor.
5. **Serve:**
   - Ladle the hot Tofu Miso Soup into individual serving bowls.
   - Garnish with thinly sliced green onions.
6. **Enjoy:**
   - Tofu Miso Soup is traditionally enjoyed hot as a starter to a Japanese meal or as a comforting dish on its own. It's nutritious, flavorful, and versatile, allowing for customization with additional ingredients like mushrooms or spinach.

This recipe is simple yet flavorful, highlighting the clean taste of tofu combined with the savory richness of miso. Adjust the amount of miso paste according to your taste preferences for a milder or stronger miso flavor.

Age-dashi Tofu Soup

Ingredients:

- 1 block (about 14 oz) firm tofu
- Cornstarch or potato starch, for coating tofu
- Oil, for frying (vegetable oil works well)
- 4 cups dashi broth (Japanese fish and seaweed stock)
- 1/4 cup soy sauce
- 2 tablespoons mirin (Japanese sweet rice wine)
- 1 tablespoon sugar
- 1 tablespoon grated daikon radish (for garnish)
- 1 tablespoon thinly sliced green onions (for garnish)
- Shredded nori (seaweed), for garnish
- Optional: Grated ginger, for garnish

Instructions:

1. **Prepare Tofu:**
    - Cut tofu into cubes, about 1-inch in size. Pat dry with paper towels to remove excess moisture.
    - Coat each tofu cube lightly with cornstarch or potato starch.
2. **Fry Tofu:**
    - Heat oil in a deep frying pan or pot over medium-high heat (about 350°F or 175°C).
    - Carefully add tofu cubes to the hot oil in batches, frying until golden brown and crispy on all sides. Remove and drain on paper towels.
3. **Prepare Broth:**
    - In a medium pot, combine dashi broth, soy sauce, mirin, and sugar. Bring to a simmer over medium heat.
4. **Serve:**
    - Place a few pieces of fried tofu into individual serving bowls.
    - Ladle the hot dashi broth over the tofu cubes in each bowl.
5. **Garnish:**
    - Garnish each bowl with grated daikon radish, thinly sliced green onions, shredded nori, and optionally, grated ginger.
6. **Enjoy:**
    - Serve Age-dashi Tofu Soup immediately while hot. The crispy texture of the tofu contrasts beautifully with the savory dashi broth, creating a delightful umami-rich dish.

Age-dashi Tofu Soup is typically served as an appetizer or side dish in Japanese cuisine, showcasing the versatility and delicate flavors of tofu when paired with a flavorful broth. Adjust the seasoning and garnishes according to your taste preferences for a personalized dining experience.

Satsuma-jiru (Satsuma Soup)

Ingredients:

- 1 lb thinly sliced pork belly or pork shoulder
- 1/2 medium daikon radish, peeled and sliced into rounds
- 1 carrot, peeled and sliced into rounds
- 1/2 kabocha squash, peeled, seeds removed, and cut into chunks
- 4 cups dashi broth (Japanese fish and seaweed stock) or chicken broth
- 1/4 cup soy sauce
- 2 tablespoons mirin (Japanese sweet rice wine)
- 1 tablespoon sake (Japanese rice wine)
- 1 tablespoon sugar
- 1 block firm tofu, cut into cubes
- 4-6 shiitake mushrooms, sliced
- 1 bunch spinach, washed and trimmed
- 4 green onions, thinly sliced (for garnish)

Instructions:

1. **Prepare Pork and Broth:**
    - In a large pot, bring dashi broth (or chicken broth) to a simmer over medium heat.
    - Add thinly sliced pork belly or pork shoulder to the simmering broth. Cook until pork is no longer pink, about 5-7 minutes.
2. **Add Vegetables:**
    - Add daikon radish, carrot, and kabocha squash to the pot. Simmer for about 10 minutes, or until vegetables start to soften.
3. **Seasoning:**
    - Add soy sauce, mirin, sake, and sugar to the pot. Stir to combine. Adjust seasoning to taste.
4. **Add Tofu and Mushrooms:**
    - Add tofu cubes and sliced shiitake mushrooms to the pot. Simmer for another 5 minutes.
5. **Finish with Spinach:**
    - Add spinach to the pot and cook until wilted, about 1-2 minutes.
6. **Serve:**
    - Ladle the hot Satsuma-jiru into individual serving bowls.
    - Garnish with thinly sliced green onions.
7. **Enjoy:**
    - Serve Satsuma-jiru hot as a main dish, accompanied by steamed rice. The rich flavors of the pork and vegetables meld together in the savory broth, creating a comforting and satisfying soup.

Satsuma-jiru is a regional specialty known for its wholesome ingredients and robust flavors. Adjust the ingredients and seasonings according to your taste preferences for a personalized Satsuma Soup experience at home.

Hamaguri Ushio-jiru (Clam Soup)

Ingredients:

- 2 lbs fresh clams (such as littleneck or Manila clams), scrubbed and cleaned
- 4 cups dashi broth (Japanese fish and seaweed stock) or water
- 2 tablespoons sake (Japanese rice wine)
- 1 tablespoon soy sauce
- 1/2 teaspoon salt (adjust to taste)
- 2 green onions, thinly sliced (for garnish)
- Optional: Thinly sliced ginger or yuzu peel (for additional flavor)

Instructions:

1. **Prepare Clams:**
    - Scrub the clams under cold running water to remove any grit or sand. Discard any clams with broken shells or that do not close when tapped.
2. **Cook Clams:**
    - In a large pot, bring dashi broth (or water) to a boil over medium-high heat.
    - Add clams to the boiling broth. Cover and cook for about 3-5 minutes, or until all the clams have opened. Discard any clams that do not open after cooking.
3. **Seasoning:**
    - Add sake, soy sauce, and salt to the pot. Stir gently to combine. Adjust seasoning to taste.
4. **Serve:**
    - Ladle the hot Hamaguri Ushio-jiru and clams into individual serving bowls.
5. **Garnish:**
    - Garnish each bowl with thinly sliced green onions.
6. **Optional Flavorings:**
    - For added depth of flavor, you can add thinly sliced ginger or yuzu peel to the broth during cooking.
7. **Enjoy:**
    - Serve Hamaguri Ushio-jiru hot as a starter or side dish. Enjoy the delicate sweetness of the clams combined with the savory umami of the broth.

Hamaguri Ushio-jiru is a light and refreshing soup that is perfect for showcasing the freshness of seafood. It's typically enjoyed in Japan as part of a traditional meal or as a comforting dish during colder months. Adjust the seasonings and garnishes according to your preference for a personalized Clam Soup experience at home.

www.ingramcontent.com/pod-product-compliance
Lightning Source LLC
LaVergne TN
LVHW081318060526
838201LV00055B/2353